Hippocrene Dictionary and Phrasebook

AUSTRALIAN

D0885635

Hippocrene Dictionary and Phrasebook

AUSTRALIAN

Helen Jonsen

HIPPOCRENE BOOKS
New York

For information, address:
HIPPOCRENE BOOKS, INC.
171 Madison Avenue
New York, NY 10016

*Library of Congress
Cataloging-in-Publication Data*
Hippocrene dictionary and
phrasebook, Australian /
Helen Jonsen.
p.   cm.
ISBN 0-7818-0539-2
1. English language—
Australia—Terms and Phrases.
2. English language—Australia
—Glossaries, vocabularies, etc.
3. Americans--Travel
—-Australia—Handbooks, manuals,
etc. 4. Australianisms.
I. Title.
PE3601.Z5J63   1997
427'.994'03—dc21   9 7-17343
                                    CIP
Printed in the United States of
America.

For our third wallaby,

Hayley

CONTENTS

Introduction

Make the decision. Head Down Under! It is a wonderful place to travel alone and even more wonderful for families. Australians believe in leisure like no other people on earth. They think everyone deserves a good time in life, every day, not just on vacation. So, for the traveler, it's imperative to enjoy yourself. Enjoy the sunshine, the sea and the beaches, the great outdoors, and the creative arts such a place breeds.

To see Australia compares with touring The United States (properly that is). You need time. When people travel to America they want to take in the big cities, some historic sights, and maybe the national parks. You need time to go from place to place, possibly covering thousands of miles. You cannot experience New York or Washington in a day, no more than you can hike through

Yellowstone and Yosemite in the same time.

An Australian trip needs to stand alone, not squeezed in between three days in New Zealand, a weekend in Bali and a side trip to Fiji. You need time to absorb the splendor of Sydney Harbour, the historic freshness of Melbourne, the living ocean museum of the Great Barrier Reef, the vastness of The Outback, the warmth of the Southern sun, the unimaginable cleanliness and welcome feeling of cities like Perth and Adelaide, a chance to sample wines and the freshest of seafood, and loll about on endless never-crowded beaches.

When it comes to language, Australians know something we don't. They watch American television and have a good ear for American-English. Many unsuspecting Yanks may not realize Aussies speak a whole other version of the Queen's English. In their fun-loving way, Aussies are not above **taking the mickey out** of a novice ear.

Here's an example: **"Can I bot a chewie?"** regardless of the accent, stands out as an odd question and the meaning will befuddle most Americans. It's the first completely Australian sentence I ever heard and it sent me looking for more. In Australian-English, **bot a chewie** means "have (*borrow to keep*) a piece of chewing gum." **Chewie** is never called gum in Australia because a **gum** is a tree!

This book will help explain the colloquialisms (not the accents) of **fair dinkum** Aussie speech.

For anyone familiar with British-English, some of the phrases will not sound strange because Aussies employ many Britishisms in their day-to-day speech. Many factors shaped the spoken language of Oz and her unique literature as well. Australia's isolation before mass media (up to the 1950s and 60s) had a heavy impact; so did its early beginnings as a prison colony—home to lower classes of British society—complete with the jargon and slang of the back alleys of London, Dublin and Glasgow. In addition, native Aborigines salted the tongue with their words and phrases to describe the things no white man had ever seen. It all adds up to a combination of factors different from those that sculpted America's English.

The Australians call their home "The Lucky Country" and travelers who get the chance to tour the world's biggest island should consider themselves lucky as well. Don't forget a **swag** full of Aussie-English and enjoy the trip all the more.

How to Use This Book

Part One offers a brief introduction to Australia's history and culture. Part Two is made up of two dictionaries: American-English and Australian-English. Part Three, the phrasebook, gives you a better feeling for Aussie words and how they are used. It groups phrases by topic. For the most part, the phrasebook offers translations of vocabulary that differ in Aussie-English, from their American counterparts. "In the Shops" offers reverse listings as well. All Australian words are boldface.

As for grammar, the Australians capitalize less than we do. A word that originated as a brand name does not retain its status as a proper noun. In colloquial speech, articles are often omitted. Ex: **"He's in hospital."** not *in the hospital.*

In the dictionaries, individual words and some phrases are listed, some as they would be spoken, others followed by articles. If you're looking for a particular phrase try both.

For example:

	show-off (person)
	show off (to)
or	big smoke, the
or	I'm buying!
	buy a round of drinks

For most phrases, look in the dictionary under the most obvious word that starts the phrase. In some cases, the phrases are too cumbersome for this simple dictionary form. In that case, you may look under specific topics in Part Three.

The Phrasebook offers groups of phrases pertaining to similar topics, particularly those of interest to a traveler. In the phrase sections, you'll find the Aussie words in bold.

Rhyming Slang: The (RS) found after words and phrases denotes rhyming slang, the Aussie equivalent of Cockney rhyming slang. It's where a word or group of words are denoted by a rhyme—usually a common phrase. Sometimes the rhymes are euphemisms covering up some unpleasantry, but more often than not, they're just a bit of fun thrown into the language. Certainly, they will confuse the uninitiated. They become even more of a problem when the actual rhyming word is dropped and a partial phrase retains the meaning. An example: *tit-for* is short for *tit-for-tat* which rhymes with *hat* . So put on your tit-for and go outside!

Spelling: Things to remember: Australian-English follows the British spellings. Color is *colour.* Favor is *favour.* Defense is *defence.* Many more examples fill the newspapers but you should be able to follow them without using a reference book.

Clipped Words: To comprehend the colloquial differences, we must understand the basics of how the Aussie mind thinks.

The fundamental rule: **if the word is long—perhaps two syllables or more— clip it and add a "y" sound!**

Perhaps the simplest and most obvious example of this is the word *Australians.* Along with the rest of the world, citizens of The Lucky Country call themselves *Aussies,* pronounced with a "zee-zee" sound.

We've already seen a few examples of this **"clip-it-plus-y"** syndrome in our sample conversation. *Tinnies* comes from tin-cans-of-beer shortened to tin cans and turned into tinnies. The game of Australian Rules Football or Aussie Rules—not soccer, not rugby—is never called by its real name in Melbourne, the country's *footy* capital. Melburnians say *footy* and that's that!

Aboriginal words: Aboriginal-based words, animal names, place names, etc. are integral parts of Aussie-English. For the purposes of the dictionaries they are not singled out. Some explanations can be found in the phrasebook.

Strine: The word strine has generally come to mean Aussie slang. The word itself is a colloquialism popularized by an author who rewrote the language the way it sometimes sounds—not the way it should be written. Where does the word *strine* itself come from? How about this for an explanation? If you say the word Australian in the most nasal way possible, it will begin to loose its A sounds and begin to sound like *Oz-strile-yan.* Condense that to *stri-yan* and stretch it into one nasally sound and you'll find *strine.* It's *Oz-as-she's-spoke, Mate!* If this all escapes you—don't worry. I prefer not to use the word strine at all because it really doesn't capture the essence of Australian English—not for Aussies and not for visiting Yanks!

Aussie animals: Some least commonly-known animals are listed in the dictionary, and so are those which have become parts of euphemisms and other colloquialisms. While most Americans associate the word marsupial, meaning pouched mammal, with kangaroos, the many species of kangaroo are only part of the more than 100 Australian marsupial species.

Part One

INFORMATION

Australia: Background & General Information

The First Fleet landed on the shores of Botany Bay, now Sydney Harbour in 1788—an event that created Australia as the world's largest penal colony, a dumping ground for the discards of British society as it was known in the eighteenth century. It also began the genocide that almost wiped the Australian Aborigines off the face of the earth.

At the turn of the twentieth century Australia became a nation of federated states governed by Parliament; but, it has not renounced its allegiance to the throne of England. The British Monarch remains the Sovereign of Australia, and the Union Jack remains prominent on the flag of The Southern Cross. While the language and culture have been based on Britain's, Australia's isolation, climate, and its lack of established classes (as in Mother England) somewhat modified its Britishness. The face of the country began to change with emigration from Meditteranean countries after the two world wars. One of the largest Greek populations outside Greece resides in Australia and the second and third most-widely spoken languages are Greek and Italian.

Finally, in 1972, Australia formally changed its racist anti-nonwhite emigration policies. Asians and Blacks were allowed to settle within the confines of its shores. This has created a new flood of emigrants, especially from Hong Kong and other Asian countries. Australia has its boat people just like America.

For the traveler, these changes add new dimensions to the Australia of today. Cities seem more cosmopolitan because of their diversity. Certainly there are more foods from which to choose. Conversations can be more lively and debate more frequent. Interest in the rest of the world has been heightened. Americans seem insular compared to Australians who fill their plate with a mix of world news, rather than local only. American newscasts, preoccupied with Washington and the hometown, do not offer as varied a fare as Australian television news. Not that Australians are particularly well read, they just seem to get more of a cross section of news from overseas.

While you travel, you will come across Australians traveling as well. Recent years have brought a big push within the country for Aussies to spend their dollars at home. Of course, there will be plenty of Germans and Japanese as well, but Aussies on holidays can make great companions and be a wealth of information. They reckon the favor will be returned someday when they or their family cross your path again somewhere down the line.

Official Stuff

The Commonwealth of Australia is a constitutional monarchy, governed by Parliament. The head of the state is Queen Elizabeth of the United Kingdom of Great Britain and Northern Ireland, who is also Queen of Australia. The Governor-general represents the Queen in Australia. The Prime Minister heads the government by leading the majority party in power in federal parliament.

There are moves to become completely independent of the United Kingdom. Some would like to remove the British Union Jack from the corner of the flag of the Southern Cross. In 2001, Australia will celebrate the centennial of the first federal parliament.

Australia is a self-governing member of the British Commonwealth of Nations and a founding member of the United Nations.

Stereotypes

Aussies do shy away from the stereotypical American—the big Yank in an alligator shirt, plaid shorts or bright green trousers who speaks loudly enough for several floors of a hotel to hear him; and, who shouts alternately, "It's just like the States!" or "We don't do it this way back home!" Get the picture?

Aussies have their stereotypes, too. "Norm" comes to mind. He's a cartoon character but you'll find him on the streets, the beaches, and in the pubs. He's the pot-bellied guy in the tank top and short shorts, wearing beach thongs and a grubby hat, who says, "'ow-yer-goin'?" and isn't looking for an answer.

Aboriginal People

One group of people have been notably left out so far—the Aborigines. Much of the relatively small population (killed off by the early settlers and European diseases) has been relegated to aboriginal reserves. Many others find themselves on the fringes of a society with which they can never truly identify. In the 1980s, pressure from civil rights groups began to give the aboriginal tribes rights to their tribal lands, among them one of Australia's greatest national attractions—Ayers Rock. The Rock in the red center of Australia is now referred to by its traditional name **Uluru**. It has been a place sacred to the aboriginal people since The Dreamtime—the time when the gods walked this earth, the time about which their creation myths were written. While the spectacle of Uluru remains accessible to the public, the local tribe has exercised its rights to declare certain areas too sacred for public display.

As Aborigines' rights become more forward in people's minds, their arts and historic artifacts are becoming more protected and more sought after. This, too, is worth noting as you tour the country.

The Sun

Australia lives by the sun and, tellingly, it has one of the world's highest rates of skin cancer. Warnings about the sun's damaging rays are serious. Something for the traveler to heed as well. A Cancer Society campaign calls for everyone to "Slip. Slop. Slap." Translated it means: slip on a shirt; slop on the sunblock cream; and slap on a hat. That's fair warning.

Children need special attention, especially at the beach where reflection off the surface of the sand or water can be as damaging as direct sunlight. Kids should not be left uncovered. While at the beach, many Aussie kids wear one- or two-piece sunsuits, which are rated for UV (ultraviolet) protection. They look like light-weight versions of wet suits. Kids think they're pretty cool. You may want them for your family. Some American catalogues carry them if you plan ahead.

When not swimming, think light-weight long shorts, long-sleeved shirts and hats with big floppy brims or "Foreign Legion-style" flaps. If they need them in Africa, you'll need them in Australia. The sun is just as strong, even when the air is cool.

Families Down Under

This could be the longest trip of your life, halfway around the world with your family in tow—an exciting vacation with so many things to plan for on the other end.

Families are welcome everywhere in Australia (probably with the exception of some four- and five-star places). Remember this is a casual country which spends a lot of time outdoors. Parks, picnic areas, playgrounds, clean outdoor restrooms or toilet "blocks," public beaches with water taps, and outdoor showers contribute to an easy stay. Theme parks and small tourist attractions lay near every major city or resort community. Sanctuaries, zoos, and nature parks draw young and old to experience the uniqueness of Australia's feathers, fur, and fins.

Part Two

THE DICTIONARIES

Legend

RS   rhyming slang

said: ...   an unofficial pronunciation

slang   when two meanings exist

see: ...   when another phrase might
   help, refers to another listing

brand   originally a brand name, now
   in common usage; Aussies do not
   usually capitalize these words

derog.   derogatory usage
   (said: ...) unofficial pronunciation

American-Australian Dictionary

Aa

a look	Captain Cook (RS)
achiever	tall poppy
Australian Capital Territory, Canberra	ACT
Australian Labor Party	ALP
afternoon	arvo
aggravated	aggro, ropeable
all or nothing	Sydney or the bush
alone	Pat Malone (RS)
aluminum	aluminium
aluminum foil	al-foil

ambulance driver	ambo
American car	Yank tank
American	Yank, Septic Tank (RS); also Septic
apartment	flat
apartment complex	block of flats
appetizer	entree
arms	Warwick Farms (RS); also Warwicks
armpit	Under the Warwick Farms (RS); also Under the Warwicks
asphalt; pavement	bitumen
Australia	Oz, the Antipodes, Terra Australis, the Land Down Under
Australian Rules Football	Aussie Rules, footy, aerial ping pong
auto body shop	panel beater
avocados	avos

Bb

baby	bub, little bub
back streets	backblocks
bad person	baddie, bad lot, nark
bald	bald as a bandicoot
baloney	bullocks, bullo, bullswool
bananas	'nanas
Bangkok, Thailand	Bangers
bangs (hair)	fringe
Baptist	Bappo
bar, saloon, tavern	pub, rubbity dub (RS), rub-a-dub (RS)
barbecue	barby
barn	shed
batter (baseball)	batsman in cricket
bed	*commonly* cot
bedroll	matilda, bluey
beer	T.T.s, tinnies, tubes, stubbies, brownies, pig's ear (RS)
bettor	punter

bicycle	pushbike
big waves	boomers
big mouth	trout mouth
biscuits	scones
blacktop, asphalt	bitumen *(said: bit-chew-men)*
blind as a bat	blind as a wombat
boondocks, the sticks, God-knows-where	boo-ay; the never-never; on the wallaby track; woop woop; back of beyond; back of Bourke; off to billy-oh; where the crows fly backwards
boots	*see*: rubber boots
borrow	to bot *(derog.)*
bottle opener	Colin Mac Donald (well-known former opening batsman) *see*: batsman
bowlegged	bandy-legged
bowling (American style)	ten-pin bowling

boy	bub, little bub
braids	plats or plaits
brawl	punch-up, stoush, box-on, barney, boil-up, blue
bread	roses are red (RS)
breakfast	brekky
bridal shower	hen's party
Brisbane	Brizzie
Brisbane residents	Brizzie boys/girls
broiler (in a stove)	griller
bucks (money)	bickies
buddy	*see:* friend
Burger King	Happy Jack's
buy a round of drinks	shout, it's my shout
B.Y.O.; a BYO	bring your own alcohol; a kind of restaurant:
B.Y.O.G.	bring your own "grog"

Cc

cafeteria	the cafe (*said: the caff*)

camper; recreational vehicle	combi; caravan
camper's kettle	billy
candy	lollies
car fenders	mudguards
car accident	prang
car registration	reggo
car trunk	boot
car hood	bonnet
cardigan	cardie
cash register	till
Catholic	Catho, mick (Irish) (*derog.*)
cheap wine	plonk, bombo
check (banking)	cheque
check-out clerk	check-out chick
cheese and crackers	cheese and greens
chewing gum	chewie
chick (girl)	sheila, bird
chicken	chook
chicken with its head cut off	headless chook
child, children	littlie(s), ankle biter(s), nipper(s) *see:* kids

chocolate	chockie
Christmas holidays	Hollies
Christmas	Chrissy
cigarette	fag
city	the big smoke
clerk	clerk (*said:* clark)
clothespins	clothes pegs
clothesline	Hill's hoist (brand)
coffee break	smoko, tea
coffee shop	coffee lounge, cafe (*said:* caff)
college, university	uni, tertiary education
coming or going, doesn't know if he's	Arthur or Martha
common-law marriage	*de facto*
common-law spouse;	*de facto*
complain, whine	whinge, flog the cat
Congregationalist	Congo
convict settlers	transportees

cook	babbling brook (RS), a snag
cookies	sweet biscuits; sweet bickies; bickies
cooler, ice chest	esky (brand)
cop	John Hop (RS)
corner store	milk bar
cornstarch	cornflour
costume	fancy dress
cotton candy	fairy floss
cowboy	stockman, jackaroo
cowboy hats	akubras (brand)
catsup	*see*: ketchup
crackers	dry biscuits; dry bickies; bickies
crayfish	yabbies
crazy	barmy as a bandicoot, crazy as a two-bob watch, kangaroos in the top paddock
crazy about, fanatical	mad keen
crib, bed	cot

cricket	a game with a bat and ball
cuddling a baby	nursing a baby
cup of coffee or tea	cuppa
curb	kerb

Dd

derby	derby (pronounced: *darby)*
desserts	sweets
diapers	napkins, nappies
dime	*(This word does not have a corresponding Aussie word.)*
diners	roadhouses
doctor's office	surgery, doctor's surgery
documentary	docco
dog	hollow log (RS)
dollar	Australian monetary unit; Oxford scholar (RS)
drive, go for a	burl

driveways	tracks (in the country)
drunk	blotto, legless, blind

Ee

elderly person	oldie, old dear, *see:* retiree
electric kettle	electric jug, birko (brand)
Englishman	Pommy, Pom
entrees	appetisers (Down Under)
environmentalist	greenie
eraser	a rubber
eucalyptus tree	gum tree
everything's great!	she's sweet, she's apples
exactly	spot on, bang on
exhausted	buggered, all in

Ff

fair chance	fair go
fan of sports	barracker
farmer, rancher	cocky, grazier, pastoralist

fenders on a car	mudguards
field	paddock
filet	fillet
fish and chips	fried fish and French fries
fish sticks	fish fingers
flashy dresser	galah
flies (bugs)	blowies
fight	*see:* brawl
float, inflatable	li-lo
flock of sheep	mob
food	tucker
football	gridiron
Fremantle, West Australia	Free-oh
French fries	chips
friend, pal, buddy	mate, digger, cobber

Gg

gal	sheila
garbage collector	garbo
gasoline	petrol
gay, homosexual	camp
gay man	camp man, poofter (*derog.*)

gelatin (like Jell-O)	jelly
girl	Barossa pearl (RS)
go-cart	billycart
Good-bye!	Cheers! Hooroo!
gossip	a stickybeak
gossip (to)	to split a bibful; put it on the bush telegraph
granola	muesli
grapevine	bush telegraph
grocery store	milk bar
gum, chewing	chewie
guy	bloke

Hh

hard candy	boiled lollies
hat	tit-for-tat (RS); also tit-fer
have a go	take a turn; have a chance
hawker, store announcer	spruiker
heating up	hotting up
hello	g'day

hiking, day hike	bushwalking, bushwalk
hobo	swagman, swaggie
home remedy	bush cure
honest	fair dinkum, dinkum, dinky-di
Hong Kong	Honkers
hood of a car	bonnet
hors d'oeuvres	savories
horseman	stockman, jackaroo
host, emcee	compere
housing development	housing estate

Ii

ill	crook
I'm buying!	It's my shout!
intense (about something)	keen (on it)
it's okay	she's sweet; she's apples
it will be okay	she'll be right.
itinerant, hobo	swagman, swaggie

Jj

jelly	jam
jerk (to) a car	to kangaroo
journalist	journo
jumpers	pinafores, pinnies

Kk

kangaroo	kanga or roo
kangaroo, big males	boomers
ketchup or catsup	tomato sauce, sauce, dead horse (RS)
kindergarten	kindie, kinder (pre-school)
kids, children	billy lids (RS), ankle biters
kiwi	New Zealand flightless bird; a New Zealander
kiwi fruit	Chinese gooseberry
knickers	*(Careful! see: panties)*

Ll

lawn bowling	bowls
lawyer	solicitor, barrister
lay away	lay-by
leftovers	bubble and squeak
lefty, southpaw	molly-dooker
a look	Captain Cook (RS)
lemon soda	lemonade
lifeguard competition	surf carnivals
lifeguards	surf lifesavers
line up	queue
linens	manchester
linen department	manchester
liquor store	bottle shop, drive-in bottle shop
live-in boy or girlfriend	*de facto*
liven it up	stir the possums
living room	lounge room
lobster	crayfish
lots (of things)	heaps
lucky	tinny
luncheonette	coffee lounge

Mm

main course	entree
marking pen	texta (brand)
marsupial	pouched mammal
mayo	mayonnaise or salad cream (similar to mayo)
Melbourne residents	Melburnians
messes things up	mucks it up
messy situation	a sticky wicket
Methodist	Metho
milkman	milko
mongrel, mutt	bitser
mosquitoes	mozzies
Most Valuable Player	*see:* MVP
motorcycle gang member	bikie
motorcycle rider	biker
Mrs. (wife)	cheese and kisses (RS)
mushrooms	mushies
M.V.P.	best and fairest

Nn

napkins	serviettes
New South Wales	an Australian State (NSW)
New South Welshman	resident of New South Wales
New Zealand	Kiwiland
New Zealander	Kiwi, Enzedder
news anchorperson, newscaster	news presenter, news reader
nickel	*(This word does not mean money!)*
No way!	Not on!
no rules at all	Rafferty's rules
nonsense, funny business	bizzo
nosy body	stickybeak
not a chance	Buckley's chance
nothing to worry about	no worries; she'll be right.
nude	bols, starkers
nurse	sister, nursing sister

nurse (to), breastfeed — *This term is not used; only use* breastfeed.

Oo

oatmeal cookies — Anzac biscuits

okay, it's okay — no worries; she'll be right!

outhouse — dunny

outlaw — bushranger

Pp

paddy wagon — divvyvan

pal — *see:* friend

panties — knickers

parking lot — car park

Parliament — seat of government: state level and federal

pavement, blacktop — bitumen (*said: bit-chew-men*)

pen, ball-point — biro (brand)

penny — *This word does not mean money!*

peppers	capsicums
pharmacist	chemist
phone	eau de cologne (RS); Al Capone (RS) piano goanna (RS)
police, cops	John Hops (RS), johnnies
politician	pollie
pond	dam (on farm)
porch	veranda
position, place	possie
postman	postie
potato chips	crisps
pot pie	meat pie
preacher	Bible-basher
Presbyterian	Presbo, Pressbutton
present, gift	prezzie
private schools	public schools
public schools	state schools
pullover, sweater	jumper

Qq

quarter	*This word never means money.*

Queensland	an Australian state, the Banana Republic
Queenslander	Banana-bender

Rr

raft, inflatable	li-lo (brand)
ranch	station
realtor, real estate agent	estate agent
red beets	beetroot
redneck	ocker
register (cash)	till
relatives	rellies, relos
restrooms (in parks, etc.)	ablution blocks, toilet blocks
retiree	pensioner, senior cit. (*said: sit*)
rides like the wind	rides like billyo
root (for a team)	barrack
rotten smelling	on the nose, gone off
row houses	terrace houses
rubber boots	gum boots, gumbies, Wellingtons, wellies

ruffians, jerks   hoons, larrikans

Ss

sandbox	sandpit
sandwich	sanger, jaffle
Santa Claus	Father Christmas
sausages	bangers, snags
school	*see:* public/private
schoolbag	port, case
senior citizens	pensioners, oldies, old dears
shark	Noah's Ark (RS)
sheep	jumbuck
shorts	stubbies (brand)
show off (a person)	a galah
shrimp	prawn
sick, ill	crook
sidewalk	footpath
silly person	a dill, dilly (RS), Blinky Bill (RS)
Singapore	Singers
sky	apple pie (RS)
sleeping bag	*see:* bedroll
slot machines	pokies

slow poke	slow coach, drongo
snack bar	tuckshop
snakes	Joe Blakes (RS)
sneakers	sandshoes
sneakers/running shoes	trainers, runners
soaking wet	wet as a shag (a marine bird)
soap	Bob Hope (RS)
soda	softdrinks
South Australia	an Australian state (S.A.)
southpaw	molly-dooker
spongy cloth	wettex (brand)
spouse, mate	china plate (RS)
squash	pumpkin
stag party, bachelor party	buck's party, buck's night
stained glass	leadlight
stand proud	sit up like Jacky
state fair (in Oz)	The Royal Show
step up to	to front (*ex:* front the till)
stewardess	hostess, hostie

strine	Aussie lingo (*see: How To Use This Book*)
stupid person, an	bunny, drongo, raw diot (sarcastic) prawn
suit	bag of fruit (RS)
supper	tea
surfers	surfies, boardies
sweater (pullover)	jumper
sweater (with buttons)	cardie
sweatshirt	sloppy joe, windcheater
sweatsuit	track suit, trackie
swimming hole	dam
swimsuit	bathers, togs, cozzie, board shorts
Sydney	Steak and Kidney (RS)
Sydney residents	Sydneysiders

Tt

takeout food	takeaway food
Tasmania	an Australian state (TAS), Tassie

tattle (to)	to pimp
tattletale	pimp
taxi stand	taxi rank
tease	take the mickey out
television	telly
terrific	beaut, bonzer, grouse, ripper
thrilled	happy as Larry, rapt, chuffed happy as a possum...
tinned food	canned food
tins	cans
toilet; bathroom	loo
track and field sports	athletics
track suit, warm up suit	trackies
trunk of a car	boot
turtleneck	polo collar jumper, skivvy

Uu

underarms	under the Warwicks (RS)
underpants	knickers

undershirt (sleeveless)	singlet, vest
unsteady	dicky

Vv

vacation	holidays
Veterans' clubs	The RSL, Returned Services League of Australia
Victoria	an Australian state (VIC)
Volkswagen	Veedub

Ww

wait a moment	just a tick!
wander	go walkabout
waterhole	dam, bogie
waves, big waves on a beach	boomers
week from Friday	Friday week
West, the	West Australia, a state
West Australia	an Australian state (W.A.)
whine, complain	whinge

white sale	manchester sale
wife	trouble and strife (RS)
wife, as "The Missus"	cheese and kisses (RS)
wild horse	brumby
wind funnel	willy-willy
within the sound of my voice	within coo-ee
woman (chick)	sheila, bird
Woolworth's (supermarket)	Woolies
work	yakker
wrench	spanner

Yy

Yes, please!	Yes, thanks!

Zz

Z, the letter	zed

Australian-American Dictionary

Aa

ABC, the	Australian Broadcasting Commission; public television
ACT, the	Australian Capital Territory; *see:* Canberra
ALP, the	Australian Labor Party
ablution blocks	semi-outdoor restrooms in parks, etc.
Addders	Adelaide, South Australia's capital

aerial ping pong	Australian Rules Football, footy
aggro	aggravated, annoyed
Akubra (brand)	stockmen's hat
Al Capone (RS)	phone
al-foil	aluminum foil
aluminium	aluminum
all in	exhausted
ambo	ambulance worker
Antipodes	early name for Australia
ankle biter	small child (*see:* kids)
Anzacs	W.W.I soldiers, oatmeal cookies
ANZAC	Australian & New Zealand Army Corps (W.W.I)
Anzac biscuits (Anzacs)	oatmeal cookies with coconut
appetisers	second restaurant course
apple pie (RS)	sky
apples, "she's apples!"	"life's great!"

argy-bargy	argumentative
Arthur or Martha	"coming or going"
athletics	track and field sports
"Aunty"	the ABC
Aussie Rules	Australian Rules Football, footy
Aussie Battler	hardworking underdog
Aussie salute	swatting flies
Australian flag	shirttail sticking out
Australian capital	Canberra (*said: Can-bra*); The Australian Capital Territory; The ACT
avos	avocados
a wander	a walk

Bb

bab	babbler
babbling brook (RS)	cook
baby's rug	baby's blanket
back paddock	North 40

back of beyond, back of Bourke	God-knows-where
backblocks	back streets ; outer suburbs
back chat	back talk
backing dog	sheep dog
backslang	to live as a hobo
baddie, bad lot	bad guy
bag of fruit (RS)	suit
bails	part of the cricket wicket
baked beans on toast	breakfast food
bald as a bandicoot	bald
Banana-bender	Queenslander
Banana Republic, the	Queensland
bandicoot	a marsupial
bandy-legged	bowlegged
bang on	exactly, hit the nail on the head
Bangers	Bangkok, Thailand
bangers	sausages
Bappo	Baptist
barby	barbecue

barmy as a bandicoot	crazy
barney	a brawl
Barossa pearl (RS)	girl
barrack, barracker	to cheer, sports fan
barrister	lawyer
basinful of trouble	lots of trouble
bathers	swimsuit
batsman	batter in cricket
Bay bug	like a small lobster
beaut!	terrific!
beetroot	red beets
behind	a goal point in footy
berk	unpleasant person
best and fairest	most valuable player; M.V.P.
bettong	a marsupial
bibful	lots of gossip
Bible-basher	preacher
bickies	money, like bucks for dollars
big smoke, the	any city
bikers	motorcycle riders
bikies	motorcycle gang members

bilby	a kind of bandicoot
billa	water
billabong	creek runoff
billy	water pot
Billy Bluegum	koala
billycan	water pot
billycart	go-cart
billylids (RS)	kids
billy tea	camp tea
billytongs	tongs for water pot
bird	gal; chick
birko (brand)	electric kettle
biro (brand)	ballpoint pen
biscuits, bickies (food)	cookies, crackers
bitser	mongrel dog, mutt
bitumen	asphalt
bizzo!	stuff, as in "what's this business?" or nonsense
Black Stump	an imaginary place
black sauce	Worcestershire sauce

blind as a wombat	blind
Blinky Bill (RS)	silly
Blinky Bill	storybook koala
block of flats	apartment complex
bloke	guy
blowies, blowflies	flies
blotto, blind	blind drunk
bludger	a do-nothing
blue, bluey	(many meanings. see separate section)
board shorts	longer-legged swimsuits
board-boy	shedhand
boardies	surfers
Bob Hope (RS)	soap, dope
bob	a coin
bobby calf	veal calf
bodgie	1950s "greaser"
bogie	swimming hole
boiled lollies	hard candy
boiled shirt	a stuffed shirt
boil-up	a brawl
bollocks!	baloney!

bon-bons, crackers	holiday noise makers
bonnet (car)	car hood
bonzer!	terrific!
boo-ay	the boondocks
boomerang bender	tale teller
boomers	big waves or big male kangaroos
boot (car)	car trunk
bot	borrow/have
bottle-oh	bottle collector
bottle shop; drive-in bottle shop	beer & liquor store
bowler	pitcher in cricket
bowls	lawn bowling
boxing kangaroo	a sporting symbol
box-on	a brawl
brekky	breakfast
brickie	brick layer
Bring Your Own (BYO)	*see:* B.Y.O.
Brizzie boys/girls	Brisbane residents
Brizzie	Brisbane
broomie	broomhand in a shearing shed

brownies	brown beer bottles, beer
brumby	wild horse
bub, little bub	baby or little boy
bubble and squeak	leftovers
bucks' party	stag or bachelor party
Buckley's chance	no chance at all
bugger all	nothing
buggered	exhausted, broken
bulletin	newscast
bullo!	baloney!
bullock	to force with strength; *ex:* "Bullock your way through."
bullswool!	baloney!
bunny	"dumb bunny"
burl	leisurely drive
bush, the	the outback or in general reference—the land; countryside
bushcook	stockman's cook
bush cure	home remedy

bushie, bushman	anyone living in the bush or off the land
bushranger	outlaw
bush telegraph	the gossip grapevine
bushwalk, bushwalking	day hiking
B.Y.O., a	restaurant where you bring your own wine or alcohol

Cc

cafe *(said: caff)*	cafeteria
camp	"gay," homosexual
capsicums	peppers
Captain Cook (RS)	look
caravan	camper, RV.
cardie	cardigan
car park	parking lot
Catho	Catholic
caulie	cauliflower
check-out chick	supermarket check-out clerk
cheeky	teasing or sarcastic

Cheers!	Bye!
cheese and greens	like a cheese platter
cheese and kisses (RS)	Mrs.
chemist	pharmacist
cheque	check (banking)
cherry ripe (brand)	candy bar
chewie	chewing gum
chiko rolls (brand)	takeout snack
china plate (RS)	spouse, mate
chips	French fries
chockie	chocolate
chook	chicken
Chrissy	Christmas
clerk *(said: clark)*	clerk
clothes pegs	clothespins
cocky	farmer, rancher
coffee lounge	luncheonette, coffee shop
Colin McDonald	a bottle opener
college	private school; more often high school; never uni
combi	camper-car in one

come a cropper	have an accident; go to ruin
come good	get better
come the raw prawn	impose foolish ideas
compere	program host
Congo	Congregationalist
coo-ee!	bush call
cop the blue	get blamed
cordial	Kool Aid equivalent, concentrated fruit juice mix
cornflour	cornstarch
corro students	correspondence students
corroboree	aboriginal celebration
cot	crib, bed
cottonbuds (brand)	Q-tips (TM)
cottonwool	natural cotton for first aid, etc.
cozzie	swimsuit
crackers	holiday noise makers
crayfish	lobster

cricket	Australia's summer sport, from England, played with a flat bat and hard ball.
cricket ground	cricket stadium
crisps	potato chips
crook (I'm crook!)	sick
crumpets	similar to American English muffins
cuppa	a cup of…(usually tea or coffee)

Dd

daggy	outdated
dags	dirty wool
Dagwood dog	hot dogs on sticks; sold at carnivals
daks (brand)	pants; "Pull up your daks!"
dam	waterhole
de facto	live-in boyfriend/ girlfriend

dead horse (RS) ('orse)	ketchup (tomato sauce)
deckie	boat's deckhand
derro	derelict, vagrant
Devvy tea	Devonshire tea, tea and scones
dicky	unsteady
didgeridoo	aboriginal wind instrument
digger	buddy; miner
diggeress	miner's wife
dilly (RS)	silly
dillybag	carry sack
dingo	species of wild dog, or gutless person
dinkum	honest
dinky-di	true blue
divvy van	paddy wagon
doccos	documentaries
(the) Doctor	West Australia's coastal wind
doing the ton	driving 100 m.p.h.
doing the block	showing off
doing your block	showing anger; tantrum

Dreamtime, The	Aboriginal time of myths and legends
Driz-a-Bone (brand)	stockmen's raincoat
drongo	stupid person
dry bickies	crackers
dunnart	a marsupial
dunny	outhouse

Ee

earbasher	talks your ear off
eau de cologne (RS)	phone
echidna	spiny anteater
electric jug	electric kettle
emu	flightless bird
emu-bobbing	collecting twigs
en suite	bedroom with attached bath
entree	first restaurant course
Enzed	New Zealand
Enzedder	New Zealander
esky (brand)	ice chest; cooler

even blind Freddy could see that!

"As plain as the nose on your face!"

Ff

fag	cigarette
fair dinkum	honest
fair go	fair chance
fairy floss	cotton candy
fancy dress	costumes
Father Christmas	Santa Claus
fillet (say the "t")	filet
first floor	2nd floor; one above the street level
fish 'n' chips	fried fish and French fries
flaggie	flagman
flake	shark filet
flat block	apartment complex
flog the cat	complain lots, whine
footy	Australian Rules Football generally; rugby in New South Wales & Queensland

Free-oh	Fremantle, WA.
Friday week	a week from Friday
fringe	bangs (hair)
frog and toad (RS)	road
front as big as Myer	person with a big "facade," audacious
front the till	stand in front of the cash register; ready to pay
full as a goog	full of food, stuffed

Gg

G'day!	Hello!
galah	rosy-breasted cockatoo; *slang:* flashy dresser, show off, acting stupid
game as Ned Kelly	adventurous
garbo	garbage collector
gets into strife	finds trouble
goanna	a monitor lizard
goanna (RS)	piano

goanna salve	household remedy
golden syrup	sweet breakfast syrup
gone off	turned rotten, rank
Good on ya!	You've done well!
goog	egg
Grand Final, the	footy superbowl
grazier	rancher, farmer
greasy wool	wool with lanolin left in
greenies	environmentalists
grey ghost	parking cop, meter maid
gridiron	American football
griller, grilled	broiler, broiled
grouse!	terrific!
gum tree	eucalyptus tree
gumbies, gum boots	rubber boots

Hh

happy as a possum	very happy
happy as Larry	thrilled

Happy Jack's (TM)	Burger King
heaps	lots of
hen's party	bridal shower; girls' night out
Hill's hoist (brand)	clothesline
hire car	rental car
holidays	vacation
hollies	holidays, usually Christmastime
hollow log (RS)	dog
holly house	vacation house
home paddock	field around house
Honkers	Hong Kong
hooly-dooly!	Holy cow!
hoons	loud-mouths, ruffians
Hooroo!	Bye!
hostie; hostess	stewardess
hotting up	heating up
housing estate	housing development
How's that?	What do you think of it?
How yer goin'?	How are you?
How's your father?	(derogatory adjective)

hump bluey	carry a bedroll
humpy	mud hut

Ii

iced coffee	dessert drink with ice cream
It's my shout!	I'm buying (a round of drinks, lunch, etc.)

Jj

Jack Shay	camp pot
jackeroo (jackaroo)	stockman, cowboy
Jacky Howe	sleeveless wool shirt; *see:* singlet
jaffas (brand)	candy balls
jaffle iron	toasted sandwich maker
jaffle	toasted sandwich
jam	jam or jelly
jelly	gelatin
Joe Blakes (RS)	snakes
joey	marsupial baby
John Hops (RS), johnnies	cops
journos	journalists

jumbuck	a sheep
jumper	pullover sweater
just a tick	wait a minute

Kk

kangaroo (RS)	"screw," a prison guard (rare)
kangaroo	largest marsupial
kangaroos in the top paddock	crazy; bat in the belfry
kerb	curb
khaki (*said* car-key)	khaki
kindie, kinder	kindergarten
Kiwi	New Zealander
Kiwiland	New Zealand
knickers	panties, underpants
knickers in a knot, don't get your	angry; upset
koala	a marsupial, not a bear
kookaburra	laughing bush bird

Ll

lamington, lam	a coconut covered mini-cake; as common as cupcakes
lap rug	a throw blanket
larrikans	loud-mouth ruffians
lay-by	layaway plan
leadlight	stained glass
lemonade	lemon-flavored soda or pop
lilo (brand)	inflatable raft
littlies	little children
lollies	candy
loo	toilet
lounge room, the lounge	living room
lounge suite	matching living room furniture

Mm

mad keen	crazy about
magpie	crow-like bird
main course	main dish

make a blue	make a mistake
manchester	linens and bedding
manchester sale	white sale
mate	pal, buddy
matilda	a bedroll
meat pie	kind of pot pie
Melbourne Cup, the	Australia's top horse race
Melburnians	Melbourne residents
Merino	sheep with the finest wool
Metho	Methodist
Mick	Catholic or Irishman (*derog.*)
mickey calf	wild veal calf
milk bar	small grocery
milko, milkoh	milkman
minced (meat)	chopped meat for hamburger
minties (brand)	chewy mint candy
mister	surgeon's title
mob	flock, crowd
moleskins	bush jeans
molly dooker	lefty

more-ish	makes you want more
morning tea	coffee break equivalent
mozzies	mosquitoes
mucks it up	messes things up
mudguards	fenders
muesli	granola
mushies	mushrooms
Myer	department store chain

Nn

'nanas	bananas
napkins, nappies	diapers
nark	bad person
nasties (*said: nah-sties*)	refers to poisonous fish, insects and animals; anything nasty
Ned Kelly	legendary outlaw
netball	a version of women's basketball
never-never, the	the boondocks
never-never plan	credit plan

news presenter	anchorperson
nippers	children
no worries	nothing to worry about
Noah's (Ark) (RS)	shark
Norm	a stereotypical character
Not on!	There's no way!
numbat	a marsupial
nursing a baby	cuddling, holding

Oo

ocker	a redneck
off to Billyo	God-knows-where
on the nose	rotten smelling
opening batsman	first batter in cricket
Oxford scholar (RS)	dollar
Oz	Australia to Aussies

Pp

paddock	field
panel beater	auto body shop

pasties (*said: pah-stees*)	takeout snack, stuffed rolled dough
pastoralist	rancher
Pat Malone (RS)	alone
pavlova, pav	a meringue-like dessert
pellets	small pieces of gum
pensioner	senior citizen, retiree
petrol	gasoline
pie warmer	commercial heating oven for meat pies
pie and peas	hand-held pot pie with peas
pig's ear (RS)	beer
pikelets	kind of pancakes
pimp	tattletale
pinafores, pinnies	ladies' jumpers (dresses)
pitch	surface beneath the cricket bowler
plastic flower (RS)	shower
plats in hair	braids

platypus	an aquatic mammal
poddy calf	hand-fed calf
poddy lamb	hand-fed lamb
pokies, poker machines	slot machines
pollies	politicians
polo collar	turtleneck
Pom	a British citizen
Pommy, Pom	a British citizen, an Englishman
poofter	a "gay" man (derog.)
poon	recluse
port	schoolbag; port wine
possie (pozzie)	position, place
possum	a marsupial
postie	postman
potoroo	a marsupial
prang	an accident
prawn	shrimp
prawn cutlets	fried shrimp
Presbo	Presbyterian
Pressbutton	Presbyterian
prezzies	presents, gifts

public schools	private schools
pumpkin (butternut, etc.)	squash
punch-up	a brawl
punt (to)	to bet
punters, punting	bettors, betting
punting	betting
pure merino	top of the line

Qq

Qantas	the Australian airline
queue, queuing up	line, lining up
quid, a few quid	money in general (from the old British pound)
quokka	a marsupial
quoll	a marsupial

Rr

R.M. Williams (brand)	bush clothier
RAC; Royal Automobile Club	like AAA, with tourist info offices

Rafferty's rules	no rules to guide you
rank, taxi rank	taxi stand
rapt	thrilled
raw prawn	idiot
reffo	refugee
reggo	car registration
rellies, relos	relatives
Rice Bubbles (brand)	Rice Krispies (TM)
rides like billyo	rides like the wind
ringer	top shearer
ripper!	terrific!
roadhouse	diner (sort of)
root	(*foul slang* — Aussies *don't* root for a team!)
ropeable	fit to be tied
roses are red (RS)	bread
Royal Automobile Club (RAC)	like the triple-A
Royal Show, the	state fair
rub-a-dub (RS)	pub, the bar
rubbers	pencil erasers
rubbity dub (RS), rubbity	pub, the bar

rug	a small blanket, a throw blanket
rugby league	in Oz, the professional game (traditionally)
rugby union	the international game; traditionally amateur
rugger	nickname for rugby

Ss

S.L.C.	surf lifesaving club; volunteer lifeguards
sandshoes	sneakers
sanger	sandwich
sauce, tomato sauce	ketchup; catsup
sausage rolls	takeout snack
saveloys, savs (brand)	hot dogs
savouries	hors d'oeuvres
scones	biscuits

sea wasps, stingers	poisonous jellyfish
septic tanks (RS)	Yanks
serviettes	napkins
shag	a marine bird
shag on a rock	an outcast
she's sweet!	everything's great!
she's apples!	everything's great!
shearing shed	where sheep are shorn
shed	barn, outbuilding
sheila	woman, girl, gal, chick
she'll be right	it'll be okay
shiny bottom	clerk or secretary
shout	pay for someone's drink, your round
show, the	*see:* Royal Show
showbags	kids' sample or goodie bags from a fair
silverbeet	Swisschard
Singers	Singapore
singlet	tank top; sleeveless undershirt

sister	nurse
sit up like Jacky	stand proud; sit up and pay attention
skivvy	cotton turtleneck
sloppy joe	sweatshirt
slouch hat, slouchy	soldier's hat
smarties (brand)	like M&M's (TM)
smoko	a break from work
snag, the	stockman's cook
snags	sausages
soda	soda water
solicitor	lawyer
spaghetti on toast	breakfast food
spanner	wrench
spider	a soda fountain drink
spot on	exactly
spring rolls	egg rolls
spruiker	hawker
squash (lemon or orange)	soda
squizz	quick look
starkers	nude
state schools	public schools

station	ranch
stayed 'til stumps	stayed until the finish
Steak and Kidney (RS)	Sydney
sticky wicket	messy situation
stickybeaks	busy-bodies
stingers	poisonous jellyfish
stir the possums!	liven it up
stoush	a brawl
struth	it's the truth, an oath
stubbies (brand)	work shorts, short beer bottle
stuffed	exhausted or broken
stuffed, get stuffed!	(*foul slang*)
stumps	part of the cricket wicket
sundowner	itinerant worker
superannuation	an employer's pension pay out
surgery, doctor's surgery	doctor's office

surf carnivals	lifeguard competitions; beach-side carnivals
surf lifesaving club (S.L.C.)	volunteer lifeguards
surfies	surfers
swag it	live as an itinerant
swaggie, swagman	itinerant, hobo
sweet bickies	cookies
sweets	desserts
Sydney or the bush	all or nothing
Sydneysiders	Sydney residents

Tt

take the mickey out	tease
take a stickybeak	be nosy
takeaway	takeout food
tall poppy	well-known achiever
Tassie (Tazzie)	Tasmania
taxi rank	taxi stand, cab stand
tea	supper

tea rooms	small restaurants
telly	television
ten-pin bowling	American-style bowling
Terra Australis	Australia
terrace houses	row houses
test match	five-day-long cricket game
texta (brand)	marking pen
till	cash register
tinny	lucky
tinny, T.T.s	can of beer, traveling tinnies
tit-for-tat (RS)	hat
to dingo	to tattle
toilet blocks	free-standing public restrooms
to kangaroo	move jerkily
toey	jumpy
togs	swimsuit
tonnes	metric weight, more than a ton
tracks	driveways
trammies	tram drivers
transportees	convict settlers

treacle	sugar cane syrup (instead of maple)
trouble and strife (RS)	wife
trout mouth	big mouth
truckies	truck drivers
tubes	beer cans
tucker	food
tuckerbag	lunch bag
tuckerbox	food box
tuckshop	snack bar
turps, hit the	drink heavily, turps from turpentine
two-bob	denotes old money, like saying two cents
two-bob watch,	a cheap watch
two-bob watch, crazy as a	crazy
Tyke	Catholic (*derog.*)
tyre	tire

Uu

Uluru	Historical Aboriginal name for Ayers Rock

uni	university
uni students	coeds
up the boo-ay	the boondocks
ute, utility wagon	car/truck combination vehicle,

Vv

veedub	V.W., Volkswagen
vegemite (brand)	Aussie food spread
veranda	any porch
violet crumble (brand)	candy bar

Ww

walkabout	wander away
wallaby	a marsupial
wallaby track, on the	God-knows-where
wallaroo	a marsupial
wally grout (RS)	shout, your round of drinks
Warwick Farms (RS)	arms

wellies, wellingtons	rubber boots
wet as a shag	soaking wet, *see:* shag
wettex (brand)	spongy cloth
where the crow flies backwards	God-knows-where
whinge	complain, whine
whinger	constant complainer
white goods	major appliances
wicket	pitcher's target in cricket
willy-willy	wind funnel
windcheater	sweatshirt
windscreen (car)	windshield
windscreen wipers	windshield wipers
within coo-ee	within the sound of your voice; nearby
wombat	a nocturnal marsupial
Woolies	Woolworth's supermarket
woolshed	where sheep are shorn
woolshed hop	barn dance

woop woop	God-knows-where
wuhl-wuhl	a marsupial

Yy

yabbies	crayfish
yakker, hard yakker	work
Yank tank	big American car
Yanks	Americans
your kick	money, kitty, wallet; wherever you keep money

Zz

zambuck	first-aid attendant
zed	the letter zee

Part Three

The Phrasebook

Aussie Words: An explanation

G′day, Mate," one man says to another as he gets off the plane in Melbourne (pronounced: **Mel-bun),** Australia. "Do you have plans for the weekend? Maybe you'd like to join us for the **footy** on Saturday **arvo**. We usually leave early to get in the **car park** at the **M.C.G.** and then we get a good **possie**, split open some **tinnies** from the **esky** and have a few **sangers** before the match."

If you are a newcomer, a **Yank,** then you will need some help with this conversation. No one's trying to be **cheeky**. Aussies talk this way. Between the Aussie accent and the words slung together without a break, it's easy to get lost.

G′day, Mate — greeting between men.
Footy — Australian Rules Football

Arvo — afternoon (a contraction of sorts)
Car Park — parking lot
M.C.G. — Melbourne Cricket Ground
Possie — position (spot, space or seat)
Tinnies — tin (or aluminum) cans of beer
Esky — ice chest (from a brand name)
Sangers — sandwiches
Yank — American
Cheeky — jokingly sarcastic

If you think this is just sports jargon and these words don't really exist, be assured they do. They are part of the everyday English of Australia.

Clipped Words

Earlier, this rule was explained in the How to Use section; but, here are a few more examples of phrases that you'll run across. From the moment Australians get up in the morning, they start clipping words. They've deemed the first meal of the day **brekky.**

Even the holidays are not sacred when it comes to language. In general, Aussies refer to the Christmas season as **the hollies**. Smack in the middle of the summer, Christmas seems to have lost its formality. Many people retreat to their **holly house** for **Chrissy** since this is the big getaway time of year. The kids have **hollies** from school and most folks take their long **holiday** from work. Vacations do not exist in the nomenclature. Children look forward to **Chrissy** like kids the world over, hoping to get **prezzies** from **Father Christmas**.

These are probably enough examples to give you an idea what we mean about **"clip-it-plus-y"** but in the following pages you'll learn more about the specific uses of shortened words which describe occupations, school days, things in the house, the car and its parts.

Rhyming Slang

As explained earlier, the second colorful derivation of the Queen's English employed Down Under is **rhyming slang**.

Here's a dialogue example. Read it aloud and see if it makes sense to you.

A husband is telling his mate about taking holidays:

"Me and the **cheese and kisses** are taking the **billylids** to **Steak and Kidney** in the morning. We're leaving right after we take our morning **plastic flower** and drop the **hollow log** with the neighbours."

Are you wondering what this conversation means? See if you can make sense of it using the following rhymes:

cheese and kisses rhymes with "Mrs." (The Mrs.).

billylids rhymes with "kids" (children).

Steak and Kidney rhymes with Sydney (the Australian city).

plastic flower rhymes with shower.

hollow log rhymes with dog.

The complete translation reads as follows:

"My wife and I are taking the children to Sydney in the morning. We're leaving right after we take our morning showers and drop the dog with our neighbors."

This small list represents only a portion of the combinations spoken throughout Oz. Ready for more?

The family monikers do not end here. **Trouble and strife** doubles for **cheese and kisses** because the last word of the phrase rhymes with *wife*. **China plate** then becomes your *mate* or *spouse*. While **billylids** were defined as kids, you probably don't know that a **billylid** is a pot cover, because **billy** is a pot in which to boil water (more about those definitions later).

An **Oxford scholar** is not a person. **Scholar** rhymes with *dollar*.

Travel Words

Specifics on traveling in Australia will be found in the later section of the book: Travel Information. Here is a brief list of colloquial references or quick bits of information you may come across. All the attractions in Oz cannot possibly be listed, just the icons or their nicknames.

Australian	**American**
Adders	Adelaide, SA, capital
Australia Day	January 26th
Ayers Rock, The Rock, Uluru	located in the center of Australia in South Australia. Aboriginal land.
Bangers	Bangkok
big smoke, the	any city; from the outback you can spot a city by its smoke
bonnet	car hood
boot	car trunk

Brizzie	Brisbane (*said: briz-bin*); Queensland's capital.
campervan	camper, RV
caravan	towable camper
combi	like a mini-van camper; usually the Volkswagen kind.
En Zed (N.Z.), Enzed	New Zealand
fossicking for gems	searching for
Free-oh, Fremantle W.A.	near Perth, one-time home of America's Cup yachting events
Gold Coast	Queensland coast; home of Surfers Paradise; Oz' Miami Beach
Great Barrier Reef	world's largest marine park; along 1250 miles of Queensland coast; one of the natural wonders of the world

hire car	rental car
hiring	renting, like a car or travel gear.
Honkers	Hong Kong
Kiwi, Kiwiland	New Zealander, New Zealand
Melburnians	Melbourne *(said: Mel-bin)* residents
mudguards	car fenders
New South Wales (NSW)	state, capital Sydney
New South Welshman	person from New South Wales
Northern Territory	territory; not one of the six states.
Outback	dry rural areas, much of the country
petrol	gasoline;
Qantas	the Australian airline; historical acronym for Queensland and Northern Territory Aerial Service

Queensland (QLD)	Sunshine State; home to the Gold Coast, The Sunshine Coast; Great Barrier Reef.
RAC, Royal Automobile Club, RACQ (in Queensland), RACV (in Victoria), etc.	like AAA; tourist offices offer free guide books and information; statewide.
Red Centre, The Red	desert in the middle of Australia.
reggo *(said: rejjo)*	car registration
rock, the	Ayers Rock, Uluru
Singers	Singapore
South Australia (SA)	state; home to wine country and some of the Red Centre, Ayers Rock.
Steak and Kidney	(RS) Sydney
Sydneysiders	Sydney residents

Tasmania; Tassie	*(said: Tazzie)* island state, off East Coast; smallest state; capital Hobart; historical name: Van Diemen's Land
Tasmanian devil	small carnivorous marsupial
taxi rank	taxi stand; no hailing; you're expected to sit in the front seat with the driver! it's insulting not to.
The Green	tropical areas up north
The Red or Red Centre	central Australia's deserts
trammies	tram drivers; tram conductors
Uluru	aboriginal name for Ayers Rock
ute	utility wagon, a pickup truck

Victoria (VIC)	Garden State (meaning flowers); capital is Melbourne
Victorian	person from Victoria
West Australia (WA)	largest state; entire west coast; capital Perth
westies	people from West Australia

Money: Aussie Dollars

Australia has increased its use of coins in recent years—up to a five-dollar coin. The complaint is you can carry a lot of "change" and have the potential of loosing track of how much is really in your pocket. Be careful.

Aussie	Explanation
dollar	the Australian dollar
two-dollar note	Aussie two-dollar bill, phased out
two-dollar coin	replaced paper bills

five-dollar coin	in addition to paper bills
old money	Aussies reference to their former use of the pound-system like in Britain. Colloquialisms survive from then.
bob	any money (*former: a shilling*)
two-bob	adjective meaning cheap; similar to two cents.
quid	any money (*former: a pound*)

(Can I bot a quid?)

Food: The Tucker Bag

They say food is the universal language, but not if you have to ask for it by name: food is personal, protected by pet names in every country. The kind of food, how it is prepared, and how it is eaten reflects the nation's lifestyle and standard of living, as well as climate, history, and tradition. Australia is not different, but Australia talks **tucker**.

Tucker:	Explanation:
tucker	any food, everyday groceries
tuckerbag	a bag to carry food; lunch bag; a supermarket chain.
tuckerbox	a box for provisions; word used before coolers
tuckbox	as above
tuck-in	a hearty meal
tuckshop	a snack bar (usually at school)

Aussie Meals:	Explanation:
brekky	breakfast
morning tea	equals coffee break
afternoon tea	equals coffee break
tea	refers to family supper
afters	dessert
sweets	dessert

Eating Out or In:

Aussie Choices:	Explanation:
bangers	sausages
bangers & mash	sausage & mashed potatoes
beans on toast	canned baked beans on toast; a breakfast food
beetroot *(said: bee-troot)*	red beets, commonly sliced or shredded on sandwiches
bickies, biscuits	cookies
biscuits, bickies	cookies
black sauce	Worcestershire sauce
boiled lollies	hard candy
bubble & squeak	leftovers
bug, Balmain bug, Moreton Bay bug	small harbor lobster; sweet meat; delicacy
cheese and kisses	not edible; (RS) Mrs.
cheese and greens	a cheese platter
cheerios	cocktail franks, little hot dogs, little boys

chewie	chewing gum
chiko roll (brand)	a savory roll like a Chinese egg roll
chips	French fries
coffee lounge	coffee shop, luncheonette
cordial *(said: cor-dee-al)*	concentrated fruit drink
cracker	not food — a Christmas party favor
crisps	potato chips
crumpet	like an English muffin; different flavor
cuppa	cup of tea; sometimes coffee
Dagwood dog	hot dog on a stick!
dead horse ('orse),	(RS) tomato sauce; ketchup
Devonshire tea, devvy tea	afternoon tea with scones piled with whipped heavy cream and jam

dim sims	small stuffed Chinese wontons, usually fried
dry biscuits, bickies	crackers
fairy floss	cotton candy
fillet (*say the* "*t*")	filet
fish & chips	fried breaded filets with French fries
flake	shark, often in fish & chips
golden syrup	sugar cane syrup, instead of maple
goog	egg
iced coffee	No! This is dessert — cold coffee with ice cream.
iced tea	doesn't exist!
jaffles	sandwiches pressed in a heated sandwich iron, close to grilled cheese.
jam	either jam or jelly
jelly	gelatin

lamington	kids' treat, white cake, cut in squares, covered in chocolate syrup and coconut.
lemonade	lemon soda
lemon squash (or orange)	a pulpy lemon (or orange) soda
little boys	cocktail franks, little hot dogs
little cakes	like American muffins
lollies	candy
meat pie, a pie	hand-held pot pie, usually filled with ground beef or lamb.
muesli	breakfast granola
milk bar	the corner store, which sells takeaway as well.
pavlova	dessert, like a meringue pie
pie and peas	meat pie covered with canned peas
pikelets	like pancakes

prawns	all shrimp
pumpkin	not what you think; squash
roadhouse	diner; truck stop
salad cream	closest thing to mayonnaise; not close enough.
sangers	sandwiches
sauce	tomato sauce meaning ketchup
saveloys (brand)	hot dogs
scones	like American biscuits
silverbeet	Swisschard
silverside	similar to corned beef
snags	sausages
soya sauce	soy sauce
spags on toast	spaghetti, usually canned, on toast
spider	a fountain soda made with different flavors
sweet biscuits, bickies	cookies
sweets	anything sweet; dessert

takeaway	takeout
takeaway shop	takeout place
tea rooms	tea & dessert cafes
toasted sandwiches, plate of	several cut up sandwiches on toasted bread with only a sliver of meat, cheese or tomatoes.
tomato sauce	ketchup
treacle	sugar cane syrup instead of maple
white coffee	coffee served with the milk already in
vegemite (brand)	a yeast-extract spread for toast and crackers; as common as peanut butter

About Restaurants

Food has different names on Aussie menus, and the menus themselves appear different. The use of the word **entree** regularly confuses Americans. The Aussies use the term correctly, as opposed to U.S. restaurateurs. *Entree* has the connotation of "upon entering" or "first." Your first choice on the menu Down Under is an **entree.**

Appetisers (note the spelling) usually head the column of soups and salads. After them comes the **main course,** which is usually called the entree in America. Often, seafood or pasta can be ordered in either **main-size** or **entree-size** portions. Remember, the **entree** is smaller.

At dessert time, you will be offered **afters** or **sweets** from which to choose.

BYO: Australians enjoy eating out (although it is not cheap). In Melbourne, **B.Y.O.** (or **B.Y.O.G.**) restaurants remain popular. That's where you can bring-your-own-grog—wine or beer, usually. Sometimes, there is a "corkage" fee to cover the glasses and the waiter. You may find it hard to get into a restaurant without reservations. **Book ahead** (rarely called "reserving").

Tipping: Australian wait staffs do not live by tips. Only in the finest of restaurants, with the best of service, will patrons tip. There is no set amount. The government sets the wages and they are standard industry wages for Australia (as much as $10 an hour or more). However, most Aussies know Americans tip—so some clever waiters, especially in tourist areas, may look like their waiting for a tip. Don't worry about it. You've paid for the service in the cost of the food!

The Pub

Aussie:	Explanation:
bistro	either sit-down service in the pub or buffet style
bottle shop	pub annex; only place liquor is sold
drink driving	drunk driving laws, DWI, a serious infraction.
drive-in bottle shop	like going through a car wash to buy liquor!
hit the turps	serious drinking; turps from turpentine

hotel	historically pubs had to have accommodation; outside big cities, the hotel is the pub.
middy	a beer glass size, about ten oz.
pig's ear	(RS) beer
plonk	house wine; cheap wine
pony	beer glass size; five oz., rare.
pub	bar, short for public house
pub crawl	bar hopping
pub hours	vary from state to state; in the country meal times are set; you may not be able to get food before traditional breakfast, lunch and dinner times; ask in the area you're traveling in.

public bar	the bar area; no food.
pub service	counter food orders
rub-a-dub, rubbity-dub, rubbity	(RS) pub
shout	buy the round
schooner	15 oz. glass of beer
stubby	beer in short brown bottles
tinnies, T.T.'s or traveling tinnies	beer (from tin, now aluminum cans)
tucker	*see Food*
wally grout	(RS) shout;
wine bar	just that; not a pub

Tea, Tea, or Tea?

Scones look and taste like American biscuits. A hostess usually offers **scones** for **morning tea** or **afternoon tea**. Both rituals follow British tradition. Work stops for these breaks, so do school and sporting events.

Australians sometimes enjoy a more festive British **Devonshire tea** as well, around three or four in the afternoon. The **devvy tea** seems incongruous with most of the hot Australian climate—a pot of hot tea and scones served with heavy whipped cream and jam. Sweet! An American might prefer an iced tea to quench his thirst. He will never find it.

If a family asks you to **stay to tea**, they want you to have dinner or supper with them. Don't be confused!

In the Shops

Most tourists shop. In tourist areas, the shops are usually open every day and longer hours; but, that's not the case outside designated areas. Australia still follows the equivalent of blue laws. Every city has its own. Just ask. Food markets have different opening and closing times than clothing and gift stores.

There's no sales tax or VAT (value added tax).

Aussie to American

akubra (brand)   similar to cowboy
                      hats

Australiana	Aussie stuff and souvenirs
boardies	long surfer's shorts
cardies, cardigans	sweaters
doona (brand); doona cover	duvet or quilt; duvet cover
driz-a-bone (brand)	traditional stockman's coat; oiled cotton raincoat
footy jumper	whatever the football team wears
jumpers	pull-over sweaters
knickers	underpants
mall (*said*; maell)	pedestrian mall, shopping mall
manchester	bedding and linens
milk bar	your basic neighborhood grocery with takeaway food
moleskins	jeans made of brushed cotton

pinnies, pinafores	ladies' and girls' jumpers
polo jumpers; polo collars	turtleneck sweaters
R.M. Williams	an Aussie clothier (like an L.L. Bean)
sandshoes	sneakers
shopping centre	part of town where the stores are
singlet	tank top
skivvy	turtleneck shirt
sloppy joes	sweatshirts
thongs	rubber sandals, flip-flops
trackie	tracksuit, sweatsuit
trackies	running sneakers

American to Aussie

sneakers	sandshoes, trackies
sweater	jumper, cardie
sweatshirt	sloppy joe, windcheater
sweatsuit	trackie, tracksuit

swimsuit	bathers, togs, cozzies, swimming costumes, boardies
tank top	singlet
turtleneck	skivvy, polo jumper

Aussie Folks

"Listen, Mack." "Hey, Buddy." Americans have lots of names they use to generalize about people. Australia has them, too, but different. Here is a list of the most common ones you might hear. Some have historic reference but remain popular today.

Aussie to American

ankle biter	small child
Aussie Battler	the hard-working underdog
bible basher	preacher, minister
bloke	any guy
bub, bubby	baby, sometimes little boy
check-out chick	supermarket check-out clerk

cobber	a buddy
cocky	a farmer
digger	any guy; from diggers in the gold mines to the trenches of W.W.I
drover	cowboy
jackeroo	cowboy
jilleroo	cowgirl
little mate	boy's friend, pal
littlie	small child
mate	male reference to another; a friend
mum, mummy	mom, mommy
rellie, relo	the relatives
sheila	any gal, chick, sometimes derogatory
stockman	horseman, cowboy
swaggie, swagman	folklore; an itinerant

From the Aborigines

The word aborigine itself is, of course, not native to Australia. It stems from *ab origine,* Latin meaning "from the origin." The aborigines are like Native Americans, a collection of tribes and families who white men lumped together under one banner.

Aboriginal culture, its myths and legends, has enriched Australian language. Not only are aboriginal place names filled with history but so are many of the colloquialisms which slide off the Aussie tongue so easily. Without aboriginal languages there would be no kangaroo or koala.

The cry **"coo-ee!"** was once used to catch another's attention while walking through the bush, where you could not be seen but might be heard. "Coo-ee" originated with the aboriginals who probably mimicked a bush bird's call. Since then, modern phrases have developed.

Example: "I can't believe I missed you at the mall Saturday. You must have been **within coo-ee**" (within the sound of my voice).

Billa comes from a word meaning water. **Billy** represents much more than a boy's name in Oz. Mainly, **billy** equals a makeshift pot or tin can in which water is boiled over a campfire, usually for tea (a camp pot).

An overflowing river or creek creates

a **billabong** or a small runoff pond along its bank, a perfect calm spot to set up camp.

The **Dreamtime** is the aboriginal time of creation, it's when the gods walked the earth. All the aboriginal myths stem from the Dreamtime.

Walkabout means what it sounds like—to go walking about or **go for a wander.** But **walkabout** is connected directly with the aborigines. Something in their heritage draws them back to their traditional homeland from time to time during their lives. The call may come at any time, no matter what other commitments the person might have. It's believed they return to their ancestral land for a kind of spiritual replenishment. While the serious meaning of **walkabout** stands, the word has other connotations now. Anyone can go **walkabout,** whether to take a break for a few hours or take time off from work for a few days. Or it can just mean going **walkabout** after dinner on a lovely evening.

A **willy-willy** is a wind funnel filled with dust or sand that dances across a dry paddock, a dusty street or along a beach.

Other aboriginal-based words slither

softly through the language of the Antipodes. A **corroboree** is a celebration, a festival. The music of an aboriginal corroboree comes from the **didgeridoo** (*said: did-jer-ree-DO*), a primitive woodwind instrument that releases an eerie sort of melody. A **dillybag** serves as a small carrier sack and a **humpy** describes a crude mud brick dwelling.

Aussie Sports & Games

American team sports are different from the sports traditionally played in British Commonwealth countries. Australia plays the English games and has a few homegrown ones as well. Ironically the national pastime is not a team sport. It's horse racing and that means gambling! You can make book legally on just about anything in Oz. Even lotto and casinos have increased in popularity. But they are not sport. Since the majority of the population lives near the ocean, water sports fill a lot of leisure time. Most sporting language is international. Only unique jargon is listed here.

Aussie:	Explanation:
athletics	track and field sports

Aussie Rules	*see:* footy
Australian Rules Football	*see:* footy
barrack, barracker	to cheer for
barracker	a fan
batsman (cricket)	the batter
belly board	small foam surfboard to ride the waves
best and fairest	most valuable player
bowls; bowlers; bowling	lawn bowling
boardie; boardies	surfer; long surfing shorts
board shorts, boardies	long surfing shorts (*see: shopping*)
bowler (cricket)	the pitcher
C.G. (as in MCG or SCG)	cricket ground (Melbourne, Sydney, etc.)
cricket	all-day sport played with bat and ball; baseball's predecessor.

darby (spelled derby)	horse race
footy	**Australian Rules Football** in much of the country. Called organized chaos and **aerial ping pong**. The game has no time outs and an oversized football is always in play, kicked through goal posts to score. Started in Victoria, most popular there. In Queensland, footy can mean rugby, professional or amateur.
footy jumper	football uniform shirt; rugby shirt
Grand Final (footy)	the Superbowl of Footy
gridiron	American football
keen	fanatical

lilo	inflatable raft
lifesavers	lifeguards
Melbourne Cup	equivalent of Kentucky Derby; held in November
netball	women's basketball game; seven players
oval (cricket)	oval field where cricket is played
pitch (cricket)	the hard surface beneath the bowler
race meeting	a horse race
rugby league	traditionally professional rugby—different rules than rugby union; played in some schools.
rugby union	the international game, traditionally the amateur and school sport in Oz.
rugger (rugby)	rugby's nickname
sport (*pl.*)	never *sports*

surf carnivals	life guard competition & beach-side fairs in one
surfies	surfers
surf lifesaving club, SLC	volunteer lifeguards
ten-pin bowling	American-style indoor bowling
test match (cricket)	five-day cricket game
yachties	yachtsmen, boating enthusiasts

Travel Information

Getting around Australia doesn't hold any surprises. But if you're on a trip limited by time, less than a month, you'll want to do most of your travel arrangements ahead of time.

Visas: Americans must have visas to enter Australia.

By air: When you book your international flights, book for Australian inter-city travel as well. It may save you money.

Rental **(hire)** cars: do it as part of a

package or it can be very expensive. Baby car seats usually cost extra. American car seats are not up to Australian standards. Whether you would actually get a ticket for not using an Aussie one is a question mark.

Gasoline: **(petrol)** sold by the **litre;** costs about twice what it does in the U.S. *Tip:* multiply cost per litre by four and you'll get your approximate gallon price.

Trains: ATS tours 800-423-2880 can supply information about train passes for foreign travelers. Train travel is not very popular in Australia because it takes time. Every major city has citywide and suburban train service.

By bus: a time-consuming way to travel interstate; like its American cousin an inexpensive way to get around. Each major city has tourist tour busses. The local or state tourist information office will have details.

U.S. Phone Numbers for specific information:

— **Aussie Help Line (Australian Tourist Commission)** 847-296-4900
— free **Australian Vacation Planner Kit** 800-333-0262

— Visas:
Australian Embassy, Washington
  202-797-3000
Australian Consulate, New York
  212-408-8400

—In Australia: State travel offices:

Australian Capital Territory (ACT),
  Canberra: Canberra Tourist
  Information Centre, Northbourne Ave.
  ph: 1800-026-166

New South Wales, Sydney:
  NSW Government Travel Centre,
  19 Castlereigh St. ph 13-2077

Northern Territory, Darwin:
  Darwin Regional Tourism Association
  Information Centre,
  33 Smith St. ph: 8981-4300

Queensland, Brisbane:
  RACQ
  261 Queen St. ph: 3361-2444

South Australia, Adelaide:
  SA Tourism Commission Travel
  Centre,
  1 King St. ph: 8212-1505

Tasmania, Hobart:
  Tasmanian Travel & Information
  Centre
  corner of Davey and Elizabeth Sts.
  ph: 6230-8233

Victoria, Melbourne:
  RACV; town hall
  Swanston Walk ph: 9650-1522

Western Australia, Perth:
  WA Tourist Centre
  Albert Facey House in Forrest Place
  ph: 483-1111

Notes

By now you realize while traveling in Australia it helps to be familiar with colloquialisms so you are not left in the linguistic cold during a conversation, or watching a news bulletin or television sit com.

Australians will not expect a visiting Yank to turn a **dinky-di** Aussie phrase. Remember, they understand you probably better than you understand them.

If by the end of your stay Down Under, Aussie phrases begin to roll off your tongue comfortably, use them. Just do not abuse them by forcing an accent or too many expressions. It will sound fake and Aussies will cut you to the quick for putting on a front. If someone does **take the mickey out of you,** laugh along and the whole moment will pass with **"no worries, mate."**

Enjoy!

HIPPOCRENE DICTIONARY AND PHRASEBOOK SERIES

Each of these titles combines the best elements from a dictionary with the best elements of a phrasebook. Slim enough to fit in a pocket, each of these titles provides the reader with brief grammar instruction, a glossary — complete with pronunciation—and a collection of helpful phrases in many and varied topics. Conversion charts and abbreviated menus can also be found in many of the titles.

BOSNIAN-ENGLISH/ENGLISH-BOSNIAN
Susan Kroll
178 pages   3 3/4 x 7
0-7818-0596-1 $11.95pb   (691)

BRETON-ENGLISH/ENGLISH-BRETON
Joseph Conroy
136 pages   3 3/4 x 7
0-7818-0540-6 $9.95pb   (627)

BRITISH-AMERICAN/AMERICAN-BRITISH
Catherine McCormick
160 pages   3 3/4 x 7
0-7818-0450-7 $11.95pb   (247)

CHECHEN-ENGLISH/ENGLISH-CHECHEN
Nicholas Awde
160 pgs, 3 3/4 x 7
0-7818-0446-9 $11.95pb   (183)

GEORGIAN-ENGLISH/ENGLISH-GEORGIAN
Nicholas Awde
152 pages   3 3/4 x 7
0-7818-0542-2 $11.95   (630)

IRISH-ENGLISH/ENGLISH-IRISH
160 pgs   3 3/4 x 7
0-87052-110-1 $7.95pb   (385)

LINGALA-ENGLISH/ENGLISH-LINGALA
Thomas Anrwi-Akowuah
120 pgs   3 3/4 x 7
0-7818-0456-6 $11.95pb   (296)

MALTESE-ENGLISH/ENGLISH-MALTESE
Grazio Falzon
176 pages   3 3/4 x 7
0-7818-0565-1 $11.95pb   (697)

PILIPINO-ENGLISH/ENGLISH-PILIPINO
Raymond Barrager and Jesusa V. Salvador
192 pages   3 3/4 x 7
0-7818-0451-5 $11.95pb   (295)

All prices subject to change. TO PURCHASE
HIPPOCRENE BOOKS contact your local bookstore, call
(718) 454-2366, or write to: HIPPOCRENE BOOKS, 171
Madison Avenue, New York, NY 10016. Please enclose
check or money order, adding $5.00 shipping (UPS) for the
first book and $.50 for each additional book.

Also from Hippocrene . . .

POLISH PHRASEBOOK AND DICTIONARY SET
Iwo C. Pogonowski
252 pages   5 ½ x 8 ½
0-7818-0134-6 $11.95pb   (192)
Vol. I: 2 Cassettes
0-7818-0340-3 $12.95   (492)
Vol. II: 2 Cassettes
0-7818-0384-5 $12.95   (486)

RUSSIAN PHRASEBOOK AND DICTIONARY
Erika Haber
256 pages   5 ½ x 8 ½
0-7818-0190-7 $9.95pb   (597)
2 Cassettes
0-7818-0192-3 $12.95   (432)

UKRAINIAN PHRASEBOOK AND DICTIONARY
Oleg Benyukh
256 pages   5 ½ x 8 ½
0-7818-188-5 $11.95pb   (028)
2 Cassettes
0-7818-0191-5 $12.95   (042)